Information Systems Engineering Library

Using CRAMM with SSADM

LONDON: HMSO

Acknowledgements

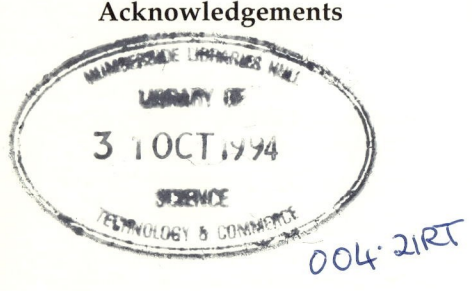

Mr Paul Turner of BIS Information Systems Ltd, under contract to CCTA, is acknowledged for technical advice on SSADM.

© **Crown Copyright**

Applications for reproduction should be made to HMSO

First published 1994

ISBN: 0 11 330629 6

For further information regarding CCTA products please contact:

CCTA Library
Rosebery Court
St Andrew's Business Park
NORWICH
0603 704930

Foreword

The **Information Systems Engineering Library** provides guidance on managing and carrying out Information Systems Engineering activities. In the IS life cycle, Information Systems Engineering takes place once the IS strategy has been defined. It is concerned with the development and ongoing improvement of information systems up to the operational stage, when systems become the responsibility of infrastructure management.

The Information Systems Engineering Library builds on guidance in the CCTA IS Guides, particularly Set A: Management and Planning Set and Set B: Systems Development Set and complements other CCTA products, in particular the project management method, PRINCE, and the systems analysis and design method, SSADM.

Volumes in the Information Systems Engineering Library are of interest to varying levels of staff from IS directors to IS providers, helping them to improve the quality and productivity of their IS development work. Some volumes in this library should also be of interest to business managers, IS users and those involved in market testing, whose business operations depend on having effective IS support by means of Information Systems Engineering activities.

The Information Systems Engineering Library also complements other related CCTA publications, particularly the IT Infrastructure Library for operational issues and the IS Planning Subject Guides for strategic issues.

CCTA welcomes customer views on Information Systems Engineering Library publications. Please send your comments to:

Customer Services
Information Systems Engineering Group
Rosebery Court
St Andrew's Business Park
NORWICH NR7 0HS

ID tokens.

Contents

Chapter		Page
	Foreword	3
1	**Introduction**	7
	1.1 Background	
	1.2 The purpose of this volume	
	1.3 Audience	
	1.4 Support available	
	1.5 Structure of this volume	
2	**Overview of the SSADM–CRAMM interface**	11
	2.1 Overview of SSADM	
	2.2 Overview of CRAMM	
	2.3 Principles of the interface between SSADM and CRAMM	
3	**Project issues**	19
	3.1 Product breakdown structure	
	3.2 Organisation and roles	
	3.3 Management meetings	
	3.4 Project initiation	
	3.5 CRAMM in a development environment	
4	**Using CRAMM with SSADM**	29
	4.1 Introduction	
	4.2 Project initiation	
	4.3 Feasibility Study Module	
	4.4 Requirements Analysis Module	
	4.5 Requirements Specification Module	
	4.6 Logical System Specification Module	
	4.7 Physical Design Module	
5	**Continuing with CRAMM**	57
	5.1 Testing and documentation	
	5.2 Post-Implementation Reviews	
	Bibliography	59
	Glossary	61
	Index	67

Using CRAMM with SSADM

Chapter 1
Introduction

1 Introduction

1.1 Background

SSADM Version 4 (hereafter referred to as SSADM) is a mature method for the development of IT based Information Systems. It was developed by CCTA and is the preferred government method.

CRAMM (CCTA Risk Analysis and Management Method) is a method for identifying and justifying all the protective measures to safeguard the security of IT systems used for processing valuable or sensitive data. CRAMM was developed by CCTA, and is also a preferred government method. One of its objectives is to be applicable to both existing and developing systems.

Assessing risk and considering appropriate security measures early in the development cycle ensures that proposed solutions take full account of security requirements, including security policy guidelines, in a cost-effective manner. Indeed, security considerations may be an important factor in choosing the best system option. Therefore, the ability to assess risk to the security of a system and incorporate countermeasures as the system is being designed and developed has significant benefits.

In particular, SSADM practitioners should be aware of the contribution that CRAMM can make to systems developed using SSADM.

1.2 The purpose of this volume

The volume aims to describe how CRAMM may be applied during a system development being undertaken under SSADM. Its objectives are to:

- provide an overview of the interface

- describe key factors in managing and undertaking a development using SSADM and CRAMM together

- give a structure to how the two methods can interact.

It should be noted that, as SSADM and CRAMM are

applicable in a broad range of situations, how they are used together will vary depending on the development being undertaken. Consequently it is important that the relationship between the two methods is carefully considered at the outset.

This volume should not be considered a substitute for the documentation on the two methods. The manuals available are listed in the bibliography.

1.3 Audience

This volume is aimed at:

- experienced SSADM practitioners who need to understand the use of CRAMM within an SSADM development project

- project managers producing project plans for an SSADM development who need to allocate the resourcing necessary to consider the risk analysis and risk management aspects of the project

- experienced CRAMM practitioners who need to understand what is required of CRAMM within an SSADM project.

1.4 Support available

SSADM is a non-proprietary, publicly available method. The private sector is encouraged to offer training, consultancy and general support facilities to SSADM users both inside government departments and in the private sector. Consequently there is now available a wide range of SSADM support services in an open, competitive market.

CCTA has licensed a number of marketing and distribution agents for CRAMM documentation and software, all of whom provide a comprehensive CRAMM support and training service.

The benefits to be achieved through the use of SSADM and CRAMM in a development project will be increased by their use within the framework provided by a recognised project management method such as PRINCE. PRINCE is CCTA's project management method which is recommended for use in government. Readers are directed to the bibliography for more details on PRINCE and its interfaces with CRAMM and SSADM.

1.5 Structure of this volume

This volume comprises:

- an overview of the SSADM–CRAMM interface, including brief summaries of the two methods

- a chapter on the key issues and management of the interface

- documentation on interfacing CRAMM with SSADM

- a short chapter on using information generated during SSADM–CRAMM reviews in subsequent operational system CRAMM reviews.

Using CRAMM with SSADM

2 Overview of the SSADM–CRAMM interface

2.1 Overview of SSADM

SSADM was developed by CCTA in 1980 as a method for carrying out the feasibility, analysis and design phases of an IT development project.

SSADM is structured into a series of self-contained Modules which overlay seven Stages, as follows:

Module	Stage	Stage Name
Feasibility Study	0	Feasibility
Requirements Analysis	1	Investigation of Current Environment
	2	Business System Options
Requirements Specification	3	Specification of Requirements
Logical System Specification	4	Technical System Options
	5	Logical Design
Physical Design	6	Physical Design

Each Module forms a distinct unit for management purposes, with a defined set of products and activities, a finite lifespan and an organisational structure. Each Stage is made up of pre-defined Steps which are further sub-divided into Tasks.

A range of techniques is used to take the broadest possible view of the system under development.

The fundamental principles behind SSADM are:

- that a sound logical design is completed and shown to satisfy business needs before any attempt is made to consider and define a physical implementation

- the use of three 'views' of the system which model the requirement from the different viewpoints of processing, events and data

- a requirements orientation, setting requirement objectives which can be explored through analysis and used to measure success

- strong user orientation, emphasising user role objectives and exploring issues of user interaction with the system

- clear management control points, which show where management need to make decisions on a project. These points, documented via the Information Highway, can be used to define contact between SSADM and other methods such as CRAMM.

2.2 Overview of CRAMM

CRAMM was developed as a method for identifying and justifying all the protective measures necessary to protect IT systems used for processing valuable or sensitive data.

The basic CRAMM procedure is known as the CRAMM review. This involves the repeated use of a software package to construct, maintain and process a security database. The use of this software package is facilitated by the use of objective questionnaires and guidelines.

- stage 1: what requires protection above a 'baseline' (code of good practice) level?

- stage 2: what and where are the security risks?

- stage 3: how can the risks be managed?

In summary these are established by:

- stage 1:
    - physical asset identification and valuation(s)
    - software asset identification and valuation(s)
    - data asset identification and valuation(s)

- stage 2:
    - assessment and rating of threats to, and vulnerabilities of, assets which are then combined with asset values to produce measures of risks

- stage 3:
    - identification and selection of countermeasures commensurate with the measures of risks calculated in stage 2.

As stated earlier, the method is supported by a software package which reflects the three stages described above. However, it is important that the output is interpreted by an experienced security analyst to ensure that appropriate reports are produced for project management. The package includes a scheduler which assists with the planning of reviews.

2.3 Principles of the interface between SSADM and CRAMM

The aim of providing an interface between SSADM and CRAMM is to assist users of SSADM to give due and timely consideration to the security requirements of systems throughout their life cycle. The two methods are discrete, but may be linked at appropriate points.

This is consistent with the SSADM view that all requirements be defined in both functional and non-functional (measures of success) terms. Thus, aspects of the new system impacting on security and back-up should be identified and documented throughout SSADM. CRAMM will provide a significant contribution in this area and will enhance the quality and rigour of the SSADM Requirements Catalogue.

The immediate value of the interface between the two methods lies in the ability to assess risk and consider appropriate security measures earlier in the development process than is often the case. The long term value lies in the ability to review security consistently throughout the life cycle of the resulting IT system. When evaluating possible options for a systems solution, it may be that the greater risk or the greater cost of protecting the system are important factors in deciding between options. Furthermore, it is easier and less costly to incorporate countermeasures early in the development of the system rather than adding them to a completed system.

There are four major points within SSADM at which CRAMM reviews should be considered. Figure 1 gives an overview of the interface, showing where in an SSADM project these points are.

In summary, CRAMM reviews can be undertaken to assist with:

- the generation of countermeasures relevant to the evaluation of Feasibility Options, if a Feasibility Study is undertaken

- the selection of a Business System Option, within the Requirements Analysis Module

- the production of the Requirements Specification, within the Requirements Specification Module, particularly in terms of agreeing systems objectives

- the selection of a Technical System Option, within the Logical System Specification Module.

In addition to the formal CRAMM reviews, SSADM projects will benefit from the rigorous way that CRAMM pursues risk analysis and management between these review points. Further details on this are given in chapter 4 of this volume.

Chapter 2
Overview of the SSADM–CRAMM interface

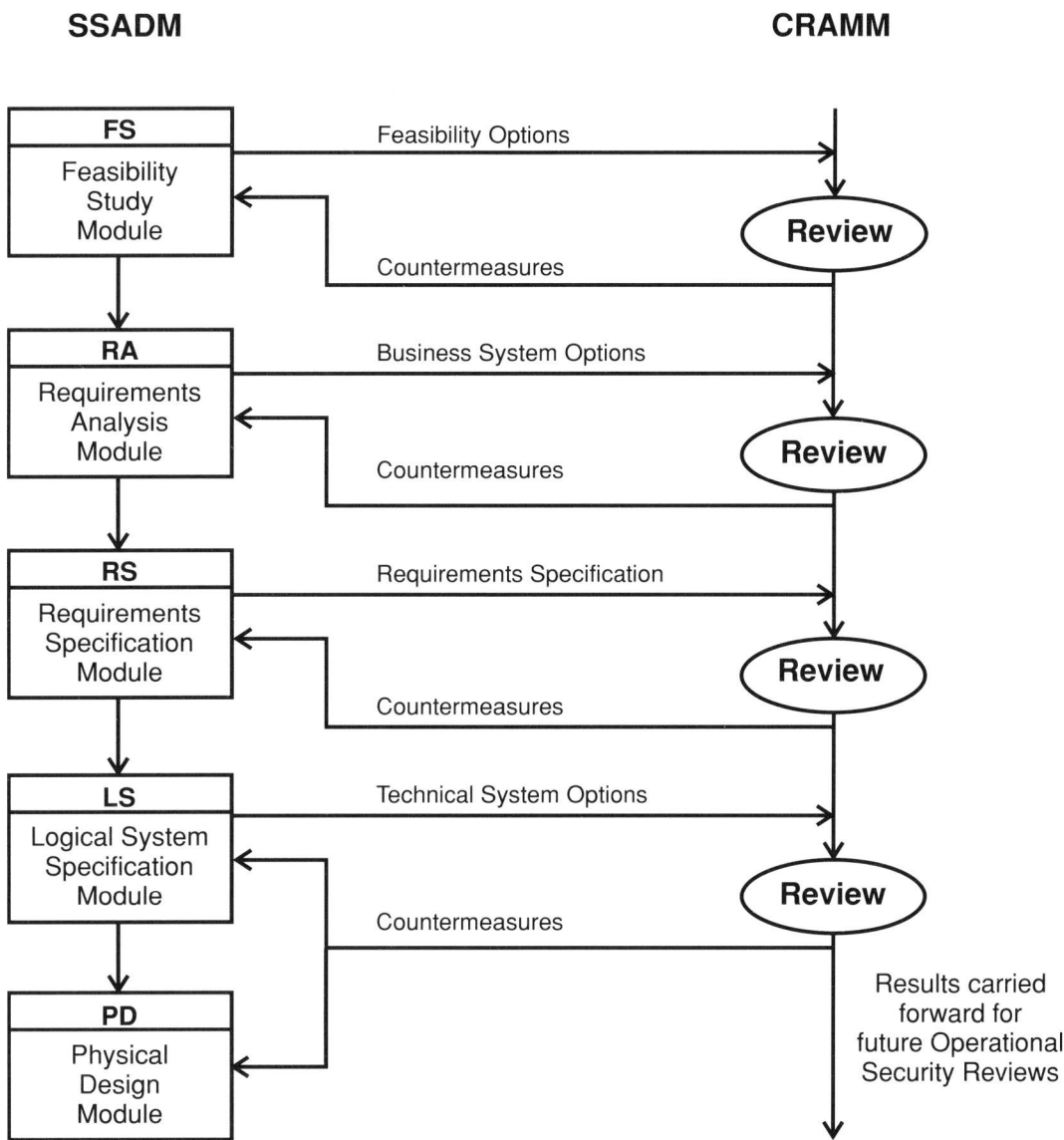

Note : The SSADM Requirements Catalogue provides the key interface to CRAMM

Figure 1: Relationship between SSADM Modules and the four CRAMM reviews

Using CRAMM with SSADM

Countermeasures recommended by CRAMM reviews should be incorporated at the relevant point of the system life cycle, which may be within the SSADM life cycle but may also be later. For example, countermeasures relating to the physical security of the computer room are outside the scope of SSADM.

In line with the modular nature of SSADM, the CRAMM reviews may be undertaken in isolation or refined and developed as the development life cycle progresses. The CRAMM software interface has been designed to give the user maximum assistance with the transfer of information between reviews. This will enable the CRAMM review process to be iterative as the development project progresses.

A CRAMM review may be undertaken on each of the options investigated during SSADM using whatever information is known, or can reasonably be assumed, about the system as it would be developed under each option. Thus the security implications of any option can be assessed and form part of the quantifiable decision criteria when selecting one option. Recommended countermeasures can be generated for each option at any point in SSADM, although it may be more appropriate to use the countermeasures summary in the CRAMM Management Report to make an initial comparison between options.

Although the information relevant to a CRAMM review may be limited early in SSADM, the CRAMM user (hereafter called 'the reviewer') nonetheless has access to, and should complete, the full range of questions used to value assets and assess threats and vulnerabilities. The reviewer may well already know more about the system than strictly required by SSADM (for example, because the site of the computer installation is already determined), and should in any case attempt to answer all relevant questions as best they can with the information available. It is recognised that SSADM may be used in a wide variety of development environments and, therefore, the degree of certainty of much of the information required for a CRAMM review will be variable.

Chapter 2
Overview of the SSADM–CRAMM interface

However, a word of caution; in section 2.1 it was mentioned that one of the fundamental principles of SSADM is that a sound logical design is completed and shown to satisfy business needs before any attempt is made to consider and define a physical implementation. Great care should be taken that the requirement of CRAMM for an 'educated guess' about uncertain aspects of the developing system should not be allowed to restrict the range of options considered in the Business System and Technical System Options Stages of SSADM. Such a restriction would be against the spirit of the method and might in some cases mean that a beneficial solution to the users' needs is overlooked.

A comprehensive set of countermeasures from CRAMM will be available from each CRAMM review. The SSADM development team, in conjunction with the CRAMM reviewer, must decide after each review which countermeasures should be incorporated into the emerging specification immediately and which should be deferred to a later stage of the development.

Using CRAMM with SSADM

3 Project issues

3.1 Product breakdown structure

The SSADM–CRAMM interface itself has been deliberately designed as a high-level interface which leaves the manager and the practitioner to address the finer issues relating to the actual production of products and control of the work. It is clearly important that those involved in using the two methods together (particularly managers) have a good understanding of the principles of both methods, particularly in terms of approach and products of each method. Much of the rest of this volume concentrates on the approach, or process, required to interface the two methods. SSADM is a product oriented method and it is important to see how the output from CRAMM fits in.

SSADM includes a hierarchy, called a Product Breakdown Structure (PBS), which is used to establish the products to be produced. The products of CRAMM will fit into this model in two ways.

Firstly, the products from each CRAMM review (which are lists of recommended countermeasures and a management report) will be entries in the general PBS, under the heading of Security Products. (Details of Security Products can be found in the Programme and Project Management Library Volume: *PRINCE User's Guide to CRAMM*.)

Secondly, these CRAMM Security Products will generate requirements which will affect other SSADM products. For example, certain CRAMM countermeasures will generate requirements in terms of how the system will be operated and thus will have an impact on one or more of the Operations Products, such as the Communications Environment or Operating Guide. The SSADM repository for all requirements is the Requirements Catalogue, supported by the relevant documentation produced when specific requirements are modelled in more detail by other SSADM techniques such as Function Definition. In principle, the requirements from CRAMM would be entered and documented in this catalogue and then fed through to SSADM products by the SSADM development process. Care should be taken to ensure that requirements documented in this way are defined in both functional and non-functional terms.

3.2 Organisation and roles

When SSADM and CRAMM are used together on a development project, there will be two teams working in parallel. The SSADM team will take the dominant role of these two teams (as it will be undertaking the majority of the work). However, as covered later in this chapter, it is likely that CRAMM reviews will be on the critical path of activities whilst they are being undertaken. Therefore, careful planning is required to integrate CRAMM activities with SSADM activities. The principles of project organisation apply to the CRAMM team in the same way as they do for the rest of the project, in that the project roles of Project Board, Project Manager, Project Assurance Team and a working team are all required. (Further information on this is available in the CCTA volume: *Managing CRAMM Reviews using PRINCE*.)

The managers of the project must identify how these roles will be filled for any particular project, giving due consideration to:

- the extent of the CRAMM work required
- the relevant experience of project participants in using CRAMM
- the need to manage and review the CRAMM work in the same way as other facets of the project
- ensuring that when information is passed between the CRAMM and SSADM teams it is interpreted and used correctly.

The resulting organisation could vary from the extremes of having a whole separate organisation for the CRAMM work that interfaces on a formal basis with the SSADM project organisation, to employing an experienced CRAMM practitioner as a part-time member of the overall project team.

3.3 Management meetings

However the project organisation is set, it is important that management meetings take place to discuss the outcome of each CRAMM review. The number, scope and timing of such meetings should be flexible and will depend on the scale of the project.

As CRAMM will produce a whole range of countermeasures, some of which will not be relevant to the current SSADM work, it is important that these meetings be properly structured to:

- give an overview of the results of the review

- discuss in detail particular countermeasures that need to be incorporated in the current SSADM work, particularly in terms of those which will need to be developed as an integral part of the SSADM project

- highlight any key areas for the future where the CRAMM recommendations may be pointing the development in a certain direction.

Where a series of high-level reviews have been undertaken to compare options (such as Business System Options), the areas where CRAMM is implying a significant security impact on a choice of option must be brought out.

3.4 Project initiation

Much of the tone of how the two development teams will interact will be set when the project is initiated. This extends to the detail of how the work will be carried out, including project scheduling, as well as the organisational and management requirements set out above. These issues are discussed in the next section.

Using CRAMM with SSADM

3.5 CRAMM in a development environment

3.5.1 Project scheduling and timing

It is important when using CRAMM within an SSADM project to plan the activities required by the two methods together to avoid unnecessary delay to the overall project. It will be necessary to hold an initial meeting between the SSADM project team and CRAMM reviewer(s) to agree a detailed project schedule.

Particular issues to resolve will include:

- how interview programmes will be scheduled (see section 3.5.4)

- how the results of each CRAMM review will be incorporated into the SSADM products (see section 3.5.5)

- timing of the CRAMM reviews, in particular identification of the points at which the CRAMM reviews must be completed to avoid delay to the development. This is discussed in the following paragraphs.

Situations where the project is held up waiting for the completion of CRAMM reviews can occur, but should be minimised where possible. Tight control of the CRAMM tasks is, therefore, necessary. Scheduling of CRAMM work will need to be done in conjunction with SSADM planning, and is preferable to use the overall project management process to control the CRAMM tasks. This can be achieved using PRINCE, the project management method developed by CCTA. The management of CRAMM reviews using PRINCE is described in the CCTA volume: *Managing CRAMM Reviews Using PRINCE*.

Whenever CRAMM reviews are carried out, the SSADM development team will require the results quickly. To assist with speeding up the CRAMM reviews, consideration should be given to:

- undertaking the CRAMM reviews at an

Chapter 3
Project issues

appropriate level of detail to avoid undue delay to the project. While it is necessary to identify physical, data and software assets at all times for CRAMM to produce meaningful asset valuations and security requirements, there is considerable flexibility in the level of detail to which this may be done. It may be appropriate, for instance, to restrict CRAMM to a minimum set of physical assets (eg 'mainframe', 'terminals' and 'network') and just one data group embracing all data to be on the system

- commencing the CRAMM review work as early as possible rather than waiting until the full set of SSADM products are finalised. In theory, the guidance on the points at which CRAMM reviews should be undertaken or updated, as given in chapter 4, specifies particular SSADM Steps and Tasks. In practice, there should be some flexibility in this, and to avoid delaying the SSADM project, CRAMM work for a particular stage may start as soon as information is available. For instance, section 4.3 indicates that CRAMM at SSADM Feasibility Study starts with setting the CRAMM Review Boundary in parallel with Step 010, followed by defining assets in parallel with Step 030. In practice, CRAMM work could usually progress directly from one task to the other

- a balance between detail and time required must be struck at stage 2 of CRAMM. While all questionnaires should be completed, one for each threat-to-asset relationship, answers may be provided at an overview level, without detailed testing of the answers provided or investigation of all the possible exceptions to the answers given. As long as realistic answers are provided, the risk of biasing the assessment towards low threats which would arise if some questions were ignored, is avoided. There will be opportunities to refine and investigate issues in more detail as the project progresses towards the final CRAMM review.

Using CRAMM with SSADM

3.5.2 Reviewing multiple options

When conducting CRAMM reviews on a number of alternative development options simultaneously, scheduling implications need to be thought through carefully as the time required for the CRAMM reviews is likely to be critical. The CRAMM review schedule may require careful consideration in this situation. For example:

- the work required for some options may be speeded up by considering them as 'what-if' options, instead of full reviews

- the timing of reviews of different options may not coincide, with the start and end dates of each CRAMM task being different.

3.5.3 Dealing with limited information

CRAMM reviews of operational systems are based on factual information about the physical environment, software, data, etc. In turn, answers to threat and vulnerability questions are based on a real system and can normally be provided with a high degree of certainty.

The CRAMM reviewer in a development environment is faced with the difficulty that much of the information required will be only theoretical. There should still be users able to provide a view of the data to be held, but the exact form in which it will be held, and the physical environment, will probably need to be obtained by interviewing the project implementation team or be deduced from the emerging specification. Some of the answers will be provisional or speculative, but they should be obtained and entered into CRAMM nonetheless and refined as necessary when details become more certain at later stages of the project development.

Later parts of this volume give guidance on the approach to obtaining information at different points in the development. At stage 2 of CRAMM, questionnaire headings and some of the questions themselves give guidance on obtaining information in the face of uncertainty.

3.5.4 Interviews with users

Data owners or users will probably need to be interviewed by both the SSADM practitioner to determine their business requirements and by the CRAMM reviewer to establish asset values, and threat and vulnerability assessments.

The different perspectives each interview will bring to the understanding of the business needs is important and the requirement for both the SSADM practitioner and the CRAMM reviewer to visit data owners or users must not be compromised. If the two interviews can be conducted simultaneously, the need to visit twice will be removed and, furthermore, should help to reinforce the co-operation necessary between the SSADM practitioner and the CRAMM reviewer.

If simultaneous interviews are planned, an attempt to pool questions and areas of investigation should be made by the two interviewers. It should be noted that SSADM interviews are normally undertaken during Stage 1 of SSADM, which would be some time before the first CRAMM review is planned (assuming there has been no CRAMM review at Feasibility Study). Therefore, care should be taken to ensure that the CRAMM reviewer can be properly prepared.

There will be a need to revisit users to clarify points arising as further CRAMM reviews are undertaken later in SSADM. Again, the objectives and content of these reviews should be considered with care, with particular regard to the involvement of SSADM practitioners.

In summary, the planning of, and preparation for, user interviews will be a key area where the CRAMM reviewer and SSADM development team must work together closely.

3.5.5 Incorporating the results of a CRAMM review

On completion of a CRAMM review, the two main deliverables will be:

- the CRAMM Management Report
- recommended countermeasures.

These outputs need interpretation and analysis, as do all systems requirements. The repository for all newly identified requirements is the Requirements Catalogue and the countermeasures output from CRAMM should, in the first instance, be added to this.

The details of how this should be done must be determined by the Project (or Stage) Manager. Key factors to consider are:

- the CRAMM software output will require interpretation. Although this will principally involve the CRAMM reviewer, the reviewer must discuss the requirements with SSADM practitioners and jointly produce a list of proposals to add to the Requirements Catalogue, either in terms of new functional requirements, or as an extension to an existing requirement

- different types of countermeasures need to be incorporated into the specification at different stages of the development cycle; both because of the nature of the countermeasures and because of the possible speculative nature of some of the information on which the CRAMM review was based. Indeed, some countermeasures will only apply to one of the multiple options being considered at any particular time. How this situation is handled must be determined by the project management team.

Throughout this volume, the SSADM Steps and Tasks at which results of CRAMM reviews should be considered are documented. However, this does not override the importance of using the Requirements Catalogue as the repository of all requirements of the system.

Chapter 3
Project issues

3.5.6 Establishing the requirement

One of the key difficulties with systems development is ensuring that an accurate specification of requirements is established. This applies to security requirements as much as anything else. The problems are largely caused by the difficulties in communicating and discussing concepts, rather than with actual working practice as would be the case with an operational system. There are specific features of SSADM that help to address these difficulties and, in particular, the CRAMM reviewer should take advantage of:

- specification prototyping, which can be used within SSADM as part of the Requirements Specification Module (Step 350) to identify discrepancies and deficiencies in the user requirement

- Function Definitions, which provide a user view of the processing to be carried out by the system. Functions are defined within the Requirements Specification Module and will provide the CRAMM reviewer with the earliest view of how the system will run operationally

- User Roles, which provide a complete and coherent view of all the user roles in the system. User roles are defined within the Requirements Specification Module and will give the CRAMM reviewer an insight into what aspects of the system differing user roles may need to access.

4 Using CRAMM with SSADM

4.1 Introduction

This chapter describes the use of the interface between SSADM and CRAMM.

While it is practical to use CRAMM during part of a development, the interface has been specifically designed to ensure that practitioners can get maximum benefit when CRAMM is used through the whole development life cycle. Information collected and reviewed at an early stage can be carried forward and refined in later reviews, avoiding the need to set up a CRAMM review from scratch each time.

However CRAMM is used in a development environment, some management actions will be necessary to ensure that the CRAMM reviews are incorporated effectively in the development. These are covered in section 4.2.

Sections 4.3 to 4.7 then describe the use of CRAMM within each SSADM Module. It should be noted that there is no CRAMM review within the Physical Design Module, but it is to be expected that many of the countermeasures recommended by earlier reviews will be incorporated at this time.

4.2 Project initiation

The tasks required to ensure that the CRAMM interface works effectively are:

- incorporate CRAMM activities and products into the SSADM-based development plan

- ensure resources are available, when required, to undertake CRAMM reviews.

The CRAMM interview programme will be a critical area of planning. This has been discussed in detail in section 3.5.4.

Before interview details can be entered into the CRAMM software tool, the reviewer must set up the review by defining it as a 'developing' system. This gives access to the SSADM interface. The software then prompts the

Using CRAMM with SSADM

reviewer to set up a Feasibility Option, Business System Option, or Technical System Option. CRAMM reviews may be initiated at any of these SSADM Stages.

Subsequently the reviewer may use the 'utilities maintenance' option to copy CRAMM data files relating to one option to up to five others (three in the case of Technical System Options), or to generate Business System Options from Feasibility Options, or Technical System Options from Business System Options. Note that the number of copies available is a limit of the CRAMM software. Full details of these functions are given in the CRAMM User Guide.

4.3 Feasibility Study Module

4.3.1 Summary of the interface

The objective of a Feasibility Study is to allow an informed decision to be taken on whether to commit resources to develop a particular system. The business and technical feasibility, and potential costs and benefits, are examined as far as they can be at this point. The business problem is defined by analysing the existing system and building up a Requirements Catalogue.

Up to six Feasibility Options can then be created, each with an investment appraisal and impact analysis. A project or projects are then selected by the Project Board.

A CRAMM review will enable the security implications of each Feasibility Option to be compared, as far as possible, given the information available. Although only outline details under each option will be known, as full a review as possible should be undertaken for each option to enable a meaningful comparison to be made and to ensure that all of the security implications are identified for each option. A countermeasures list, if only in summary form, will be produced, enabling the development team to determine whether the countermeasures required for each option influences its feasibility.

Chapter 4
Using CRAMM with SSADM

4.3.2 SSADM actions

STEP 010 - Prepare for the Feasibility Study:

- as part of Task 010.20, the CRAMM Review Boundary must be agreed and documented.

STEP 020 - Define the Problem:

- the initial CRAMM study can assist in producing high level Requirements Catalogue entries and help in building the Outline Required Environment Description.

STEP 030 - Select Feasibility Options:

- the composite (Business System and Technical System) options developed in Task 030.50, are output to the CRAMM Security Review

- within Task 030.60, the cost of CRAMM Recommended Countermeasures should be assessed and incorporated as part of the investment appraisal.

STEP 040 - Assemble Feasibility Report:

- as part of Task 040.10, the CRAMM Security Review may need updating if the feasibility products are amended. Only major changes to the configuration are likely to have a significant impact

- within Task 040.20, relevant details from the CRAMM Management Report should be incorporated in the Feasibility Report. Some work is likely to be required to extract the relevant information, and it will be helpful if the project team can indicate to the CRAMM reviewer the format in which they require information. The CRAMM reviewer may then produce his own report, distilling information from the CRAMM Management Report.

The preceding discussion is summarised in figure 2 on page 32.

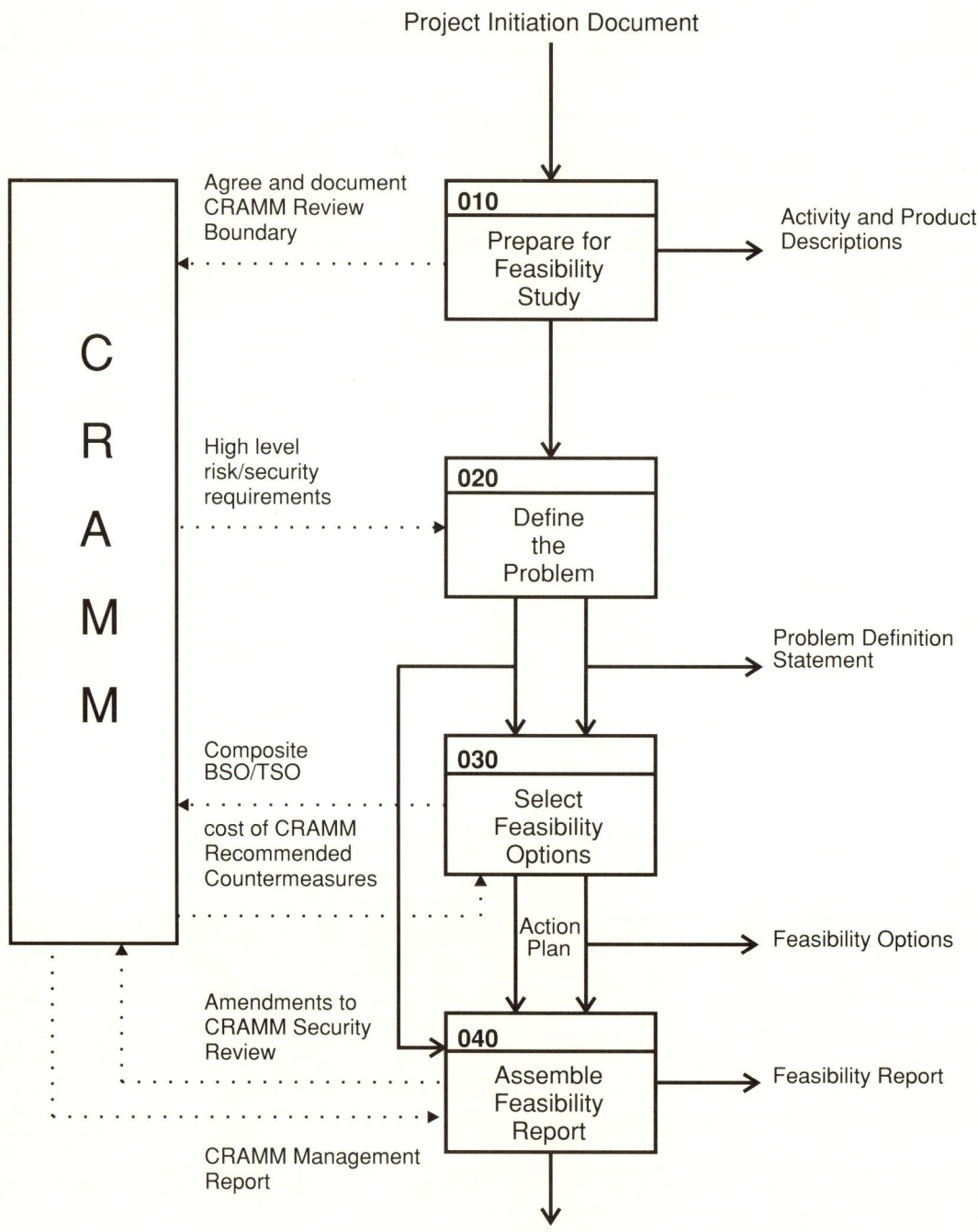

Figure 2: Relationship between CRAMM and the SSADM Feasibility Study Module

4.3.3 The CRAMM review

Each stage of CRAMM should be used, as far as possible, in the normal way to assist in the evaluation of Feasibility Options. In the light of limited information available, however, certain points should be borne in mind, as described below.

CRAMM stage 1

Establishing the Boundary of the Review
The CRAMM boundary would normally cover all hardware, software, communications, documentation, personnel, physical accommodation and environmental systems which will support the system under development. If this is not the case then the omissions should be discussed and agreed with the project manager(s).

Project Schedule
The CRAMM project schedule will depend upon a number of factors, some of which may not be known at this time. The main factors are:

- the number of data groups and hence the number of data valuation interviews

- the number of project options to be considered

- the size and complexity of the proposed technical solutions which influences the number of asset groups and the number of threat and vulnerability questionnaires which require completion.

It may be more efficient to incorporate CRAMM tasks into the overall project schedule rather than using a separate CRAMM schedule.

Identify Physical Assets
Use the Technical Environment Description in the Feasibility Options produced in SSADM to define the physical configuration of the option(s) to the CRAMM software. This will be at a high level, eg 'mainframe', 'network'.

Identify Data Assets
This step can best be completed by interviewing the potential users of the new system. All data for the

proposed system (as far as is known at this time) will be documented in the Logical Data Model, which includes entity descriptions and relationship descriptions. These are cross-referenced to data stores in the Data Flow Model in SSADM. CRAMM data assets may be defined in terms of a data store, a subset of a data store, or some combination of data stores.

The reviewer should remember that where possible data assets should be grouped together to facilitate the accurate valuation of data in a reasonable period of time. In particular, the reviewer should be aware that a separate questionnaire may need to be completed for each data asset and thus:

- too few data assets may make the valuation too coarse and may not enable sensitive components of data to be distinguished from the less sensitive components

- too many data assets may result in extra time being spent for little extra benefit.

Ensure that all data has been covered by checking that all entities have been allocated to a data asset.

Value Data Assets
It is more difficult for the reviewer to value data on a proposed system than an existing system. Much of the information will be ill-defined or unknown. For example, some of the information about the proposed system required under 'Data Details' may not be known by the interviewee including:

- origin of data

- data input

- data output

- processing steps

- files stored on magnetic media.

Chapter 4
Using CRAMM with SSADM

This information is not vital to the CRAMM software. It is used by the reviewer to set the scene for the data valuation. Even if this information is absent, it is important that the reviewer discusses each data group and its possible future use with the interviewee, carefully guiding the interviewee through the various scenarios which might arise. He/she should be prepared to prompt the interviewee with particular scenarios. The qualification of the potential impacts (the data valuation) from these scenarios must be generated by the interviewee and not the reviewer.

Value Physical Assets
The best possible approximation of the costs of the physical assets identified should be entered. These figures may well be highly tentative, but there will be opportunities to replace them with more accurate figures once actual hardware options are being considered in SSADM Stage 4 (Technical System Options).

CRAMM stage 2

The reviewer should identify all of the threat-to-asset relationships that are likely to be relevant for the system under review.

The full set of questionnaires, and questions within each questionnaire, is available to the reviewer. Every questionnaire should be completed in full even if this requires theoretical answers about the proposed development rather than answers based on an actual system. Omitting some questions at different points may lead to anomalies between reviews conducted on the same project at different times, and may result in incomplete countermeasures recommendations. A suitable interpretation may need to be placed on some questions for systems under development. This is illustrated by the following questions in the 'Vulnerability to System Infiltration by Staff' questionnaire:

- Q4: 'What is the average level of experience of staff with the system?' Answer normally 'Under one year/No experience as yet' for a developing system. However, if it is known that many of the staff have experience with a similar system to that

Using CRAMM with SSADM

implied by one of the project options, then a different answer may be appropriate

- Q5: 'Would it be comparatively easy to break out ... into the operating system ...?' The best approach may be to discuss the principle with the IT Security Officer, or other personnel who can speak authoritatively about these issues, and answer 'yes' unless they can state that such a facility would definitely not be permitted on systems within their responsibility

- Q6: 'Would any software packages from unofficial suppliers ever be installed on a trial basis?' Establish whether or not the organisation has a policy on this.

In many cases the wording of particular questions has been designed to embrace both operational and developing systems. Where the question text itself provides insufficient help, the questionnaire heading may provide some assistance in establishing the most appropriate source of information.

There are no extra questionnaires to deal specially with risks such as an unsuccessful development being aborted. Risks to the development itself are outside the scope of CRAMM except in so far as they ultimately present a risk to live data, and they are then generally covered by existing questions. One threat type ('system failure') does, however, contain alternative questions for developing systems.

CRAMM stage 3

If the proposed project option involves the use of existing assets eg hardware, software, communications, etc, then the required countermeasures should be compared against those already existing. This will enable the project team to assess the suitability of existing assets in terms of security.

If countermeasures do exist they should be added to the CRAMM software via the CRAMM stage 3 'Decisions' menu.

Chapter 4
Using CRAMM with SSADM

Some of the recommended countermeasures may not be applicable to certain options and these should be entered as 'Not Applicable' in the CRAMM stage 3 'Decisions' menu.

Make an estimate of the cost of the recommended countermeasures, as accurately as possible; enter these and print the report, which will be incorporated into the Feasibility Options investment appraisal.

Management Meetings
Some discretion should be used concerning the number of management meetings to be held. The normal pattern would be a meeting at the conclusion of each of the CRAMM stages, probably considering all of the Feasibility Options together, assuming CRAMM work progresses on them in parallel. Separate meetings for each Feasibility Option are likely to take an unjustified amount of time. For a small project with little information known at the Feasibility Study stage, it may be desirable to combine the meetings for one or more of the CRAMM stages. This will require particular care to ensure that the review is properly planned and supported by management at all stages.

Depending on the level of detail to be discussed at the CRAMM stage 3 review meeting for the Feasibility Study, the reviewer may wish to use the actual countermeasure list printed, or just the summary provided by the CRAMM Management Report.

4.4 Requirements Analysis Module

4.4.1 Summary of the interface

During Stage 1 of SSADM (Investigation of Current Environment) no CRAMM review would be carried out, although:

- the CRAMM Review Boundary should be determined as part of Step 110 (Establish Analysis Framework)

- information collected (particularly that in the Data Flow Model (DFM) and Logical Data Model (LDM)) could be passed to the CRAMM reviewer

Using CRAMM with SSADM

to assist with setting up the CRAMM review at the next stage. In this case the CRAMM reviewer should take care to ignore physical constraints as these will be removed in Step 150 (Derive Logical View of Current Services).

Stage 2 of SSADM involves identifying and selecting Business System Options for the new system. Up to six Business System Options are identified. Two or three are short-listed and a cost/benefit analysis developed. One Business System Option is selected and this is developed, within the Requirements Specification Module, into a detailed requirements specification.

CRAMM reviews can contribute to the selection of a Business System Option, by analysing the security implications of each alternative. The recommended countermeasures should be evaluated in terms of cost and the implications for the operational aspects of the proposed system and the results fed into the selection process.

4.4.2 SSADM actions

STEP 210 - Define Business System Options

- the CRAMM Security Review will be undertaken following Task 210.40, using the descriptions of the two or three selected Business System Options

- CRAMM Recommended Countermeasures from the CRAMM review will be added to the description of the Business System Options, and their costs will be incorporated in the outline Cost/Benefit Analysis of each, as part of Task 210.50.

Chapter 4
Using CRAMM with SSADM

STEP 220 - Select Business System Option

- as part of Task 220.20, CRAMM Recommended Countermeasures for the chosen option should be incorporated into the Requirements Catalogue. These countermeasures will be those particularly relevant to the protection of data against threats such as:

    - system infiltration by outsiders

    - system infiltration by staff

    - misuse of resources

    - system failure

    - user error.

Ensure that there is no duplication of requirements on the Requirements Catalogue. The project team may need assistance from the CRAMM reviewer to select and justify their choices from the recommended counter-measures.

The preceding discussion is summarised in figure 3.

4.4.3 The CRAMM review

Many of the issues to be considered when gathering data for a CRAMM review at this point, and passing the results back to SSADM, are similar to those discussed for the Feasibility Study.

At this Stage of SSADM, user requirements are defined in more detail. The main areas of concern are data and applications software. The output from CRAMM will be used primarily to assess the need for countermeasures which affect the application system itself. However, countermeasures relating to equipment or services on which the application will depend, ie recommendations for hardware, operating system and communications security should also be considered. In practice, the selection of a Business System Option may be influenced by physical and environmental security issues, as well as those relating to the application.

Using CRAMM with SSADM

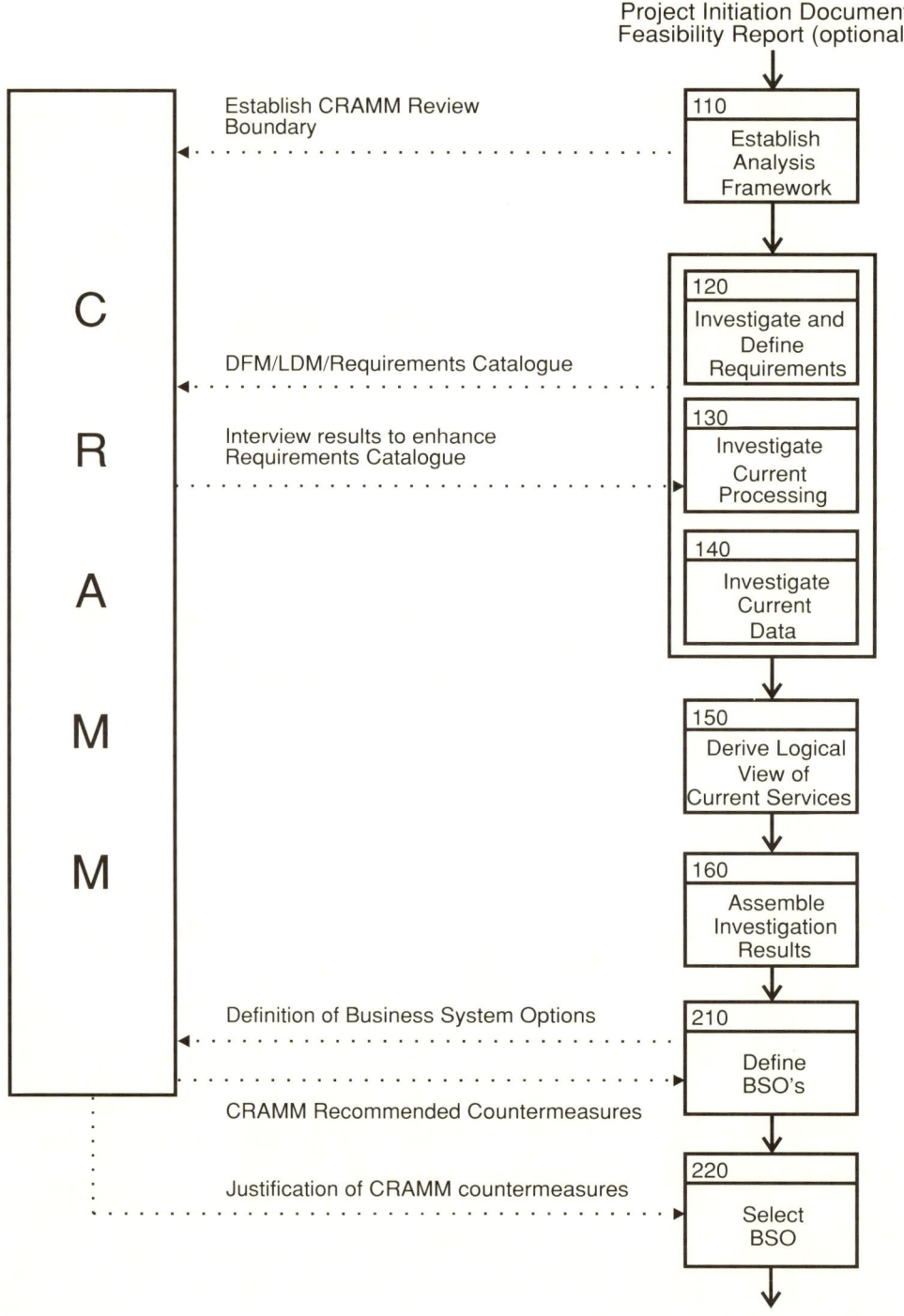

Figure 3: Relationship between CRAMM and the SSADM Requirements Analysis Module

Chapter 4
Using CRAMM with SSADM

Moreover, a CRAMM model with no physical assets will generate incomplete results. The reviewer should attempt to enter at least a broad assumption of the physical assets required for the proposed system in order to produce countermeasures which can be realistically compared.

Therefore, as at the Feasibility Study, the reviewer should enter as much information as is available, with assumptions if necessary, for the complete set of questionnaires and countermeasures. However, it is crucial that tentative decisions made at this point in SSADM are not allowed to pre-empt the development of Technical Systems Options.

Generating CRAMM Reviews

When the reviewer sets up or amends projects at this juncture, the reviewer may specify up to six Business System Options (although it is to be expected that only two or three copies will be put forward for review); the CRAMM software will set up separate reviews for each, each identified by a unique name. If CRAMM was used at Feasibility Study the reviewer may copy across any of the reviews of the Feasibility Options to any Business System Option. These may now be refined further as the specifications for each are established.

It is also possible to copy data from one Business System Option to another, and the reviewer may select whether to copy all of the data, or just some of the assets. Further details are given in the CRAMM User Guide.

CRAMM stage 1

Establishing the Boundary of the Review

While it is still necessary to scope and schedule the review properly, information on the proposed physical configuration of the system, ie the physical assets which will support the application system, is likely to be limited and need not be specified here in detail.

Identify Physical Assets

If the new development will run on existing hardware, enter details of that equipment. If the type of equipment has not been decided or is to be evaluated during the SSADM process, make a broad assumption of the physical assets required to support the system as described in the Business System option but this decision should not be allowed to pre-empt consideration of a range of Technical System Options in Stage 4 of SSADM.

Identify Data Assets
This step will probably require an interview with the systems analyst. SSADM documentation will now have been produced, including the Data Flow Model and Logical Data Model, and will give a greater degree of accuracy and detail than for the Feasibility Study. However, the approach to defining and grouping data assets is otherwise similar to that described under Feasibility Study.

Value Physical and Data Assets
The same issues arise as discussed under Feasibility Study.

CRAMM stage 2

The same approach to assessing threats and vulnerabilities should be adopted as described under Feasibility Study. A complete set of threat and vulnerability assessments should be completed. Where reviews have been carried forward from reviews at Feasibility Study, some of the details will be unchanged but should still be reviewed. It may be that little new information has been established about the physical configuration since undertaking the Feasibility Study; and the CRAMM reviewer should concentrate on threats relevant to the individual applications, such as:

- system infiltration by outsiders
- system infiltration by staff
- misuse of resources
- system failure
- user error.

CRAMM stage 3

It is possible that certain existing program modules will be used in the new system. If this is the case then any security countermeasures included in the module should be identified and compared with those recommended by CRAMM. In this way the applicability of the module in

Chapter 4
Using CRAMM with SSADM

terms of security can be assessed and the findings fed back to the project team.

If existing countermeasures do exist, they should be added to the CRAMM Software via the CRAMM stage 3 'Decisions' menu.

Some of the recommended countermeasures may not be applicable to the proposed system and these should be entered as 'Not Applicable' in the CRAMM stage 3 'Decisions' menu.

Although all the recommended countermeasures will be calculated and may be printed, in practice, the input to SSADM will principally consist of application-related countermeasures. These will mainly be those required to protect against the above threat types. Input/Output Controls and (depending on the system type) Financial Accounting Countermeasures are likely to be directly relevant. The complete range of countermeasure groups may be obtained by looking up the appropriate entries in the CRAMM User Guide.

Management Meetings
It may be appropriate to concentrate on application-related countermeasures at this time. This is likely to make the management review process more straightforward. Otherwise, similar considerations apply as at Feasibility Study when determining the number and breadth of management meetings for the CRAMM review at this SSADM Stage.

Depending on the level of detail required, the reviewer may wish to use the actual countermeasures list printed, or just the summary provided by the CRAMM Management Report.

4.5 Requirements Specification Module

4.5.1 Summary of the interface

Once a Business System Option has been selected the CRAMM Recommended Countermeasures will be incorporated in the full system definition as it is prepared.

Using CRAMM with SSADM

A completely new CRAMM review would only be undertaken at this time if either no CRAMM review was undertaken as part of the Requirements Analysis Module, or the selected Business System Option is a hybrid of alternatives originally reviewed. Even in the latter case, it is likely that the CRAMM reviewer would decide to refine one of the previous reviews.

Where CRAMM has been in use already on the project, the main emphasis here will be in revising the high level review undertaken earlier, and the incorporation of relevant countermeasures into the specification. The Business System Options considered in the Requirements Analysis Module have been studied at a high level, with the emphasis being on looking at those factors which are likely to affect the choice between options; now the chosen option is being specified in detail, with a whole range of techniques being employed by SSADM to ensure that a complete and accurate specification results. Of particular interest to the CRAMM reviewer will be the prototyping work being done, the function definitions produced and the user roles identified, as these will provide the clearest view to the users of how the system will actually operate.

Nevertheless, the comments on the CRAMM review given in section 4.4.3 are applicable to the use of CRAMM in this Module and for brevity are not repeated here. Once again, it is emphasised that the review at this point will focus on precision and detail, whereas previous reviews (whether as part of a Feasibility Study or in helping to choose a Business System Option) will have tended to concentrate on the major differences between proposed options.

4.5.2 SSADM actions

STEP 310 - Define Required System Processing:

(NB: Be aware of the requirements relating to CRAMM Recommended Countermeasures (which were accepted and incorporated into the selected Business System Option) and ensure that appropriate account is taken of these during this Stage.

Also be aware that when defined in detail, some recommended countermeasures may add a cost element that might invalidate the selected Business System Option.)

- within Task 310.30 some or all of the CRAMM Recommended Countermeasures will be incorporated in the lower-level Data Flow Diagrams as Security Processes

- within Task 310.40, the Elementary Process Descriptions will be modified to incorporate Security Processes

also within Task 310.40, ensure that countermeasures which provide control over input and output are provided for in the I/O Descriptions. To select these, print the 'Input/Output Control' countermeasures group from CRAMM's Recommended Countermeasures.

STEP 320 - Develop Required Data Model:

- some or all of the CRAMM Recommended Countermeasures will be incorporated into the Required System Logical Data Model particularly on the Entity and Relationship Descriptions.

STEP 330 - Derive System Functions:

- within this Step, incorporate the impact of Security Processes in I/O Structures.

STEP 370 - Confirm System Objectives:

- ensure all CRAMM recommended countermeasures are adequately covered in the Requirements Specification.

Using CRAMM with SSADM

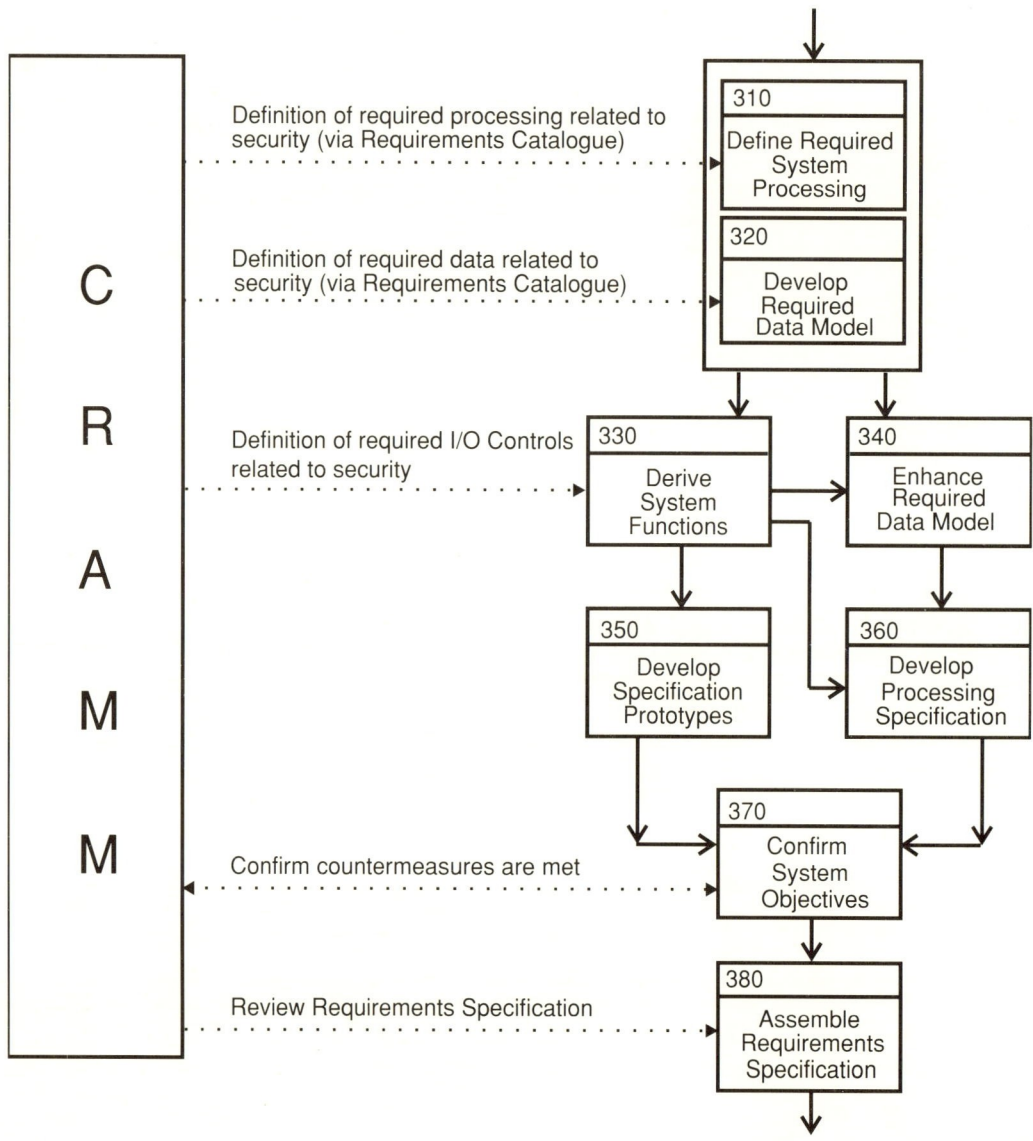

Figure 4: Relationship between CRAMM and the SSADM Requirements Specification Module

Chapter 4
Using CRAMM with SSADM

STEP 380 - Assemble Requirements Specification:

- within this Step, the CRAMM reviewer will have a role as part of the Project Team in ensuring the consistency and completeness of the specification.

The preceding discussion is summarised in figure 4.

4.6 Logical System Specification Module

4.6.1 Summary of the interface

Stage 4 of SSADM involves creating Technical System Options relating to the Requirements Specification defined in SSADM Stage 3 and selecting one of these. This is paralleled by Stage 5, Logical Design.

Up to six Technical System Options are created. These are discussed with the users and a short-list of two or three is produced. A specification of each of these is produced, including a cost/benefit analysis. A selection is made of one Technical System Option.

Of the six Technical Options, those which are rejected prior to the production of specifications are only assessed at a high level and CRAMM will not be appropriate to this decision.

The CRAMM review undertaken at Stage 4 of SSADM will provide a more refined picture of security requirements than those undertaken earlier as the information available from SSADM, although still at a logical level, is now providing a view of how the requirement will be implemented in addition to the data and processing requirements previously specified.

This will be the final CRAMM review during SSADM. Note that some countermeasures will not be incorporated in the specification (apart from being recorded in the Requirements Catalogue) until Stage 6 of SSADM, and other countermeasures may relate to requirements beyond the scope of SSADM, such as installation and staffing. This should be formally noted for consideration at a later stage.

Using CRAMM with SSADM

In Stage 5, the Installation Style Guide input into Stage 4 (and potentially developed into an Application Style Guide) will need to be reviewed for any impact arising from the selected Technical Environment Description (which may incorporate some of the CRAMM countermeasures relating to the technical environment).

4.6.2 SSADM actions

STEP 410 - Define Technical System Options:

- within Task 410.40 the Technical Environment Description (for each option) should be output to the CRAMM Security Review

- the CRAMM review will return CRAMM Recommended Countermeasures which are divided into the security aspects of:

    - hardware and software

    - communications

    - procedural

    - physical

    - personnel

    - environmental.

Countermeasure cost details should also be available. Ensure all recommended countermeasure groups not considered already are covered, and review those incorporated earlier. The Technical Environment Description should be updated to include this information:

- within Task 410.60, the CRAMM Recommended Countermeasures must be taken account of in the Impact Analysis and Cost/Benefit Analysis.

STEP 420 - Select Technical System Option:

- within Task 420.20, ensure the reworked option takes provision for the CRAMM Recommended Countermeasures

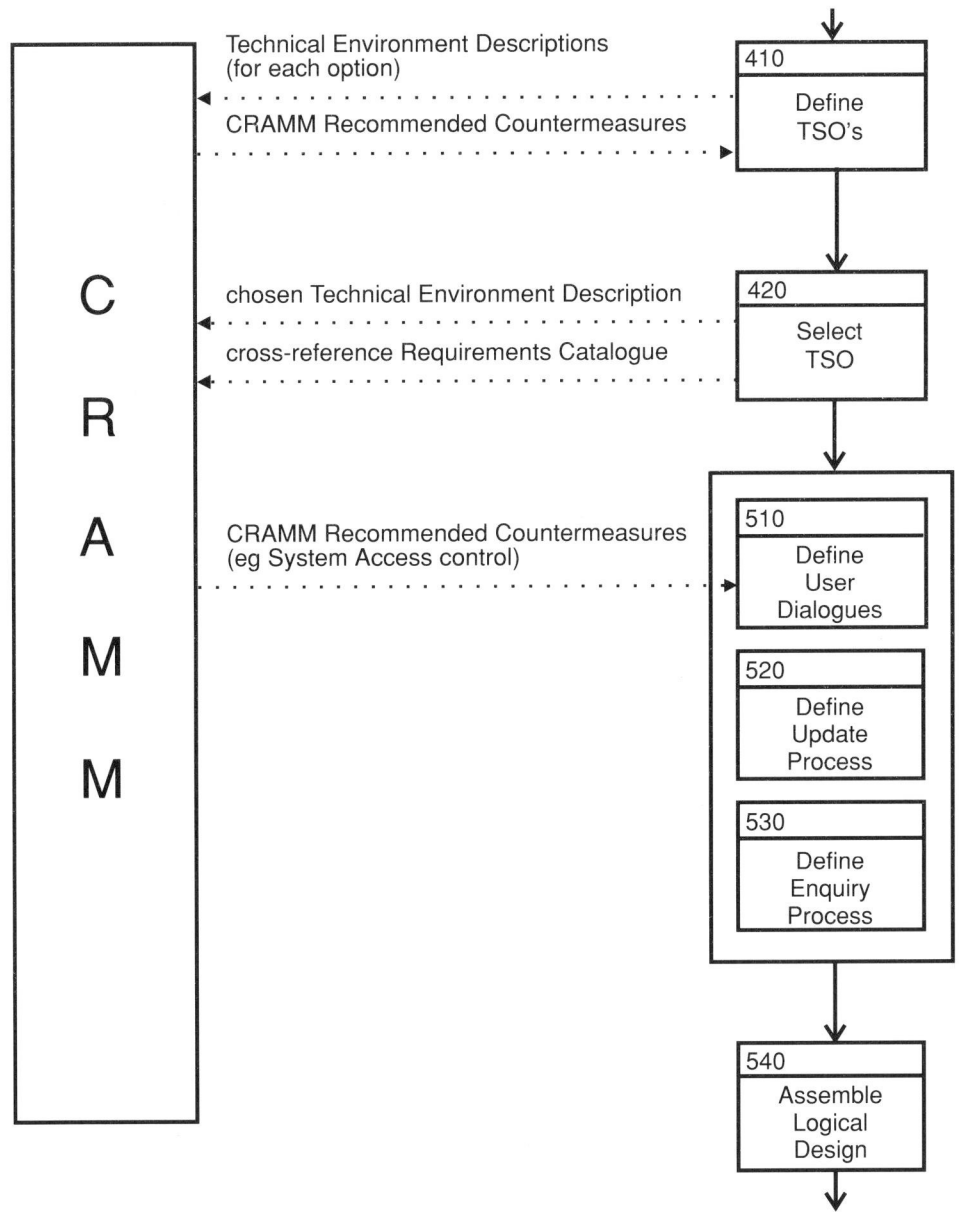

Figure 5: Relationship between CRAMM and the SSADM Logical Specification Module

Using CRAMM with SSADM

- output the selected Technical Environment Description to the CRAMM Security Review. (This is the final output to the CRAMM Security Review from SSADM and will describe the configuration on which subsequent countermeasures will be based)

- a formal review of the CRAMM Recommended Countermeasures produced during SSADM Stage 4 should be undertaken. The countermeasures to be implemented should be represented in the Requirements Catalogue. Any not previously recorded should be added now, together with proposed actions for all countermeasures. It may be appropriate to cross-reference the Requirements Catalogue to the CRAMM reports.

STEP 510 - Define User Dialogues:

- within this Step, CRAMM Recommended Countermeasures, notably those in the 'System Access Control' countermeasure group, must be considered in screen design, particularly in the provision of appropriate sign-on and menu screens. The Installation (or Application) Style Guide should be reviewed in the light of these.

The preceding discussion is summarised in figure 5.

4.6.3 The CRAMM review

At the Technical System Options Stage of SSADM, information on proposed hardware, software, communications, etc, will become available through SSADM Technical Environment Descriptions. Usually there will be a number of technical options proposed and security requirements could play a key part in the selection of an option. There are two ways in which CRAMM can be used to generate security requirements for each technical option:

- separate CRAMM models could be set up for each option, with each proposed configuration being documented, separate threat and vulnerability assessments undertaken and separate lists of recommended countermeasures produced for comparison with each other. This approach would

Chapter 4
Using CRAMM with SSADM

have to be adopted when proposed options were significantly different from each other

- a CRAMM model could be set up for the first option and then the CRAMM 'what if' facility could be used to identify any differences in security requirements between the first option and the other options. This approach would normally be quicker and simpler to use and would be appropriate in all cases except where the proposed options were significantly different from each other, eg centralised mainframe versus distributed microcomputers.

More detail will now be available regarding the physical environment than at Business System Options and the CRAMM reviewer will be able to generate additional countermeasures relevant to this.

Although the reviewer may focus on the physical environment, threats and countermeasures solely related to applications should still be considered in case the technical options under consideration imply changes to the assumptions made about data and software.

The reviewer may generate up to 3 Technical System Options; these may be set up for the first time, or copied from Business System Options and further refined. As before, it is also possible to copy data from one option to another, if separate Technical System Options are used rather than 'what-ifs' on one option.

Once one or more reviews have been set up, they should be completed as for a normal CRAMM review. All stages of CRAMM should be completed, and all relevant threats and vulnerabilities assessed, in order to generate a complete list of the countermeasures which should be incorporated into the chosen system.

CRAMM stage 1   **Establishing the Boundary of the Review**
Now that complete details of possible system configurations are available, the boundaries should be defined in detail, to ensure accuracy and consistency of treatment between alternative options.

Identify and Value Physical Assets
Precise details of equipment and replacement costs implied by each Technical System Option should be entered.

Review Data Assets
During the CRAMM review at Technical Systems Options, details of data assets and their valuations may have been copied across from the review at Business System Options. It is unlikely that data asset groupings or valuations will have changed since then but the reviewer has an option to review and amend these if necessary. However, it is important to note that changes could invalidate recommendations made as a result of the CRAMM review of Business System Options. Therefore, the implications of any such changes should be assessed carefully.

CRAMM stage 2

A comprehensive set of threat and vulnerability assessments should be completed. Where reviews have been carried forward from Business System Options reviews, some of the details (eg those relating to data or software) may be reasonably accurate but should still be reviewed. More firm and refined answers to questionnaires concerned with physical-type threats should now be obtained and entered into CRAMM.

CRAMM stage 3

Protection against some threats is likely to be directly relevant to the Technical Environment Description prepared at this Stage of SSADM. These threats include:

- system infiltration by outsiders
- system infiltration by staff
- misuse of resources
- hardware failure
- system failure
- user error.

Chapter 4
Using CRAMM with SSADM

However, many other threats, whilst not generating countermeasures for inclusion on the Technical Environment Description, may generate requirements for countermeasures which could influence the choice of Technical System Options. These should be noted for inclusion in system operating procedures.

These threats include:

- fire
- water damage
- natural disaster
- staff shortage
- wilful damage by outsiders
- wilful damage by staff
- theft by outsiders
- operator error
- application programmer error
- system programmer error
- maintenance error
- WAN operator error
- LAN operator error.

Countermeasures to protect against these threats are only likely to influence the selection of Technical System Options if they are either very expensive or would have major organisational implications. Countermeasures which do not influence selection of options will be relevant to the final installed system but these need not be considered until later in the project. However, later parts of SSADM do not generate further input to CRAMM reviews, except for refinement of details already entered. Therefore, complete information should be entered into CRAMM even if the resultant countermeasures are not immediately required.

If some of the proposed Technical System Options involve the use of existing assets, eg hardware, software, communications, etc., then the required countermeasures should be compared against those already existing. This will enable the project team to assess the suitability of existing assets in terms of security.

If existing countermeasures do exist they should be added to the CRAMM software via the CRAMM stage 3 'Decisions' menu.

Some of the recommended countermeasures may not be applicable to certain options and these should be entered as 'Not Applicable' via the CRAMM stage 3 'Decisions' menu.

Management Meetings
As with earlier stages of the development, the number, scope and timing of management meetings should be flexible and will depend on the scale of the project. The meeting(s) may be restricted to consider only physical countermeasures if there has been little change to application-related countermeasures since the review of Business System Options. It may be that only those countermeasures which are required for the Technical Environment Description need to be discussed, and those for threats such as fire, water damage, etc., discussed at a separate meeting at the final Stage of SSADM.

4.7 Physical Design Module

The Physical Design Module consists of Stage 6 of SSADM (Physical Design), which specifies the physical data, processes, inputs and outputs, using the language and features of the chosen physical environment and incorporating installation standards.

A further CRAMM review at this point should be unnecessary. To the extent that any refinements to the proposed system have an impact on security requirements, the CRAMM model for the chosen Technical System Option may be updated and a revised countermeasure list produced. However, if no significant changes are made, the countermeasures produced at SSADM Stage 4 should be incorporated, where necessary, in the final stages of development. When particular countermeasures become relevant is for the development team to decide.

Chapter 4
Using CRAMM with SSADM

The impact of Physical Design on CRAMM work, therefore, involves ensuring that the approved CRAMM recommendations are incorporated in the design documents. The SSADM development team will initially classify the physical environment in terms of the facilities and features it provides for both data and processing. The security characteristics of the proposed system may well have a significant effect on this environment and the CRAMM reviewer should contribute to this classification.

Additionally, specific countermeasures should be incorporated as appropriate during Physical Design.

Using CRAMM with SSADM

5 Continuing with CRAMM

5.1 Testing and documentation

The security requirements of the system, which will have been defined by the CRAMM reviews undertaken during analysis and design, will generate testing and documentation requirements. These requirements must be incorporated in plans for implementation of the system.

5.1.1 Testing requirements

The requirements determined as a result of the CRAMM reviews will form a basis on which to develop security test plans. The first steps in setting up such a plan are:

- define security test cases, based on the agreed CRAMM Recommended Countermeasures added to the Requirements Catalogue

- allocate responsibilities for:

    - creation of test scripts

    - scheduling of tests, including integration with other testing where necessary

    - carrying out tests and checking results

    - reviewing results and signing off the tests.

5.1.2 Documentation

The system documentation requirements will depend on installation standards, but would be expected to include:

- operating instructions, which should incorporate security procedures which satisfy countermeasures from the CRAMM Operational Countermeasures and any Protective Operating Procedures

- user manuals, which should include manual security requirements from the CRAMM countermeasures list.

5.2 Post-Implementation Reviews

Using CRAMM at appropriate points in SSADM should ensure that effective security measures are incorporated when the system becomes operational. The effective operation of these countermeasures should be tested as soon as practically possible, especially those indicated as 'Trusted Countermeasures'.

Using CRAMM with SSADM

Security is never static, new risks appear and existing risks become more or less important, and it should, therefore, be kept under constant review. The CRAMM review for whichever option was finally implemented can be used as the basis for future reviews of the system, subject to whatever refinements need to be made to reflect changes to the system over time.

The timing of the next review will be affected by factors such as the rate of change of technology, business requirements, value of data held, etc. Previous data entered will need to be checked for continued accuracy; this is likely to be considerably quicker than starting a completely new CRAMM review.

On average, the need for a follow-up review should be assessed annually even if no significant changes have been recorded, to ensure that the countermeasures based on the review data are still applicable, and that those recommended during development are still being effectively applied in practice.

It is suggested, however, that the first CRAMM review of the operational system should be carried out shortly after implementation, when the system has been 'bedded in', on the basis that:

- it will probably have been some time since the development reviews were carried out
- it is general good practice to carry out a post-implementation review after installing a new system. This applies to security as much as to other aspects of a system.

Note that CRAMM does not test the actual operation or effectiveness of the installed countermeasures, apart from an assessment of those deemed to be 'trusted' countermeasures, ie those where assurance is required that the countermeasures will always function in the manner it was designed for, in order to ensure a secure system. However, for the majority of countermeasures, testing will be a separate task not covered by CRAMM.

Bibliography

The following are either directly referred to or expand on the topics discussed in this volume.

Programme & Project Management Library

Available from HMSO bookshops and HMSO Publications Centre, details on back cover.

- Using SSADM with PRINCE
  ISBN: 0 11 330598 2

- PRINCE User's Guide to CRAMM
  ISBN: 0 11 330596 6

Methodologies

Available from NCC Blackwell, Oxford House, Oxford Road, Manchester, M1 7ED.

- PRINCE - Projects in Controlled Environments
  ISBN: 0 85554 012 6

- SSADM Version 4 Reference Manual
  ISBN: 1 85554 004 5

Available from CCTA Library, Rosebery Court, St Andrew's Business Park, Norwich, NR7 0HS.

- CRAMM – CCTA Risk Analysis and Management Method

Other publications

Also available from CCTA Library, Rosebery Court, St Andrew's Business Park, Norwich, NR7 0HS

- Managing CRAMM Reviews Using PRINCE
- An Overview of CRAMM

Using CRAMM with SSADM

Glossary

Business System Options	This SSADM product is described fully in the SSADM Version 4 Reference Manual. Within the SSADM–CRAMM interface, Business System Options are output to CRAMM to provide base data for CRAMM reviews in SSADM Stage 2.

The main information provided by the Business System Options for CRAMM purposes is the description of data, which is in terms of data stores, a Logical Data Structure and Entity Descriptions. The CRAMM reviewer will wish to re-group the data at a high level which separates data likely to have differences in value and physical environment – a different categorisation to those considered in SSADM.

Within this document, featured in Steps:

210   Define Business System Options

Cost/Benefit Analysis — Within the SSADM–CRAMM interface, the cost of countermeasures recommended by a CRAMM review will be incorporated into a Cost/Benefit Analysis.

Costs of individual countermeasures are provided in one of the countermeasure reports output by the CRAMM software. It may be that many of the countermeasures have not been given an individual cost; indeed the cost of many countermeasures is hard to establish in isolation, and may be negligible. Where costs have been established, these will have been aggregated in the CRAMM Management Report, and the total costs shown in the countermeasures section of this may be the most useful figures for the SSADM team. It is important that an estimate of the cost of a countermeasure is provided unless this cost is certain to be insignificant in overall system terms.

Using CRAMM with SSADM

	Within this document, featured in Steps:
	030 Select Feasibility Options
	210 Define Business System Options
	410 Define Technical System Options
Countermeasure	A check or restraint on the system designed to enhance security in one of the following ways:

- reduce risk (by reducing either threat or vulnerability)
- reduce the impact of an incident
- detect an attack.

CRAMM Management Report	The report produced by the CRAMM software summarising the findings of a CRAMM Security Review.
	Within this document, featured in Step:
	040 Assemble Feasibility Report
CRAMM Recommended Countermeasures	The countermeasures recommended by CRAMM to reduce the security risk to an acceptable level.
	Within this document, featured in Steps:
	030 Select Feasibility Options
	210 Define Business System Options
	220 Select Business System Option
	310 Define Required System Processing
	320 Define Required Data Model
	410 Define Technical System Options
	420 Select Technical System Option
	510 Define User Dialogues

Glossary

CRAMM Review Boundary	The boundary containing the assets of the proposed system covered by the CRAMM Review.

Within this document, featured in Steps:

010   Prepare for Feasibility Study

110   Establish Analysis Framework

CRAMM Security Review	An analysis and assessment of security risks facing the proposed system and recommendations on the required countermeasures to reduce these risks to an acceptable level.

Within this document, featured in Steps:

030   Select Feasibility Options

040   Assemble Feasibility Report

210   Define Business System Options

410   Define Technical System Options

420   Select Technical System Option

Requirements Catalogue	This SSADM product is described fully in the SSADM Version 4 Reference Manual. Within the SSADM–CRAMM interface, the Requirements Catalogue is used to record CRAMM Recommended Countermeasures and the actions/solutions for each. Some countermeasures may exist on the Requirements Catalogue for some time before being actioned, for example, those which are incorporated within Physical Design (Stage 6).

Within this document, featured in Steps:

030   Select Feasibility Options

220   Select Business System Option

420   Select Technical System Option

Using CRAMM with SSADM

Security Processes
Processes incorporated on lower-level Data Flow Diagrams as a result of CRAMM countermeasures.

Within this document, featured in Steps:

310   Define Required System Processing

330   Derive System Functions

Technical Environment Description
This SSADM product is described fully in the SSADM Manual. Within the SSADM–CRAMM interface, the Technical Environment Description is a key input to CRAMM reviews. The CRAMM reviewer will be particularly interested in:

- location (site, building, room) and whatever details are available about whether or not this will be a greenfield site or shared building. Details (eg for physical access questionnaire) may need to be clarified by the CRAMM reviewer interviewing the project team. Note that if the proposed system will be in an existing location, then full details will be available for the CRAMM review

- physical assets, which may be at a high level, such as 'mainframe' and '100 VDUs', or 'two minis' and 'network controller'. The project team should discuss with the CRAMM reviewer the amount of sizing and timing information that is appropriate for the CRAMM review. A balance must be struck to ensure that any additional effort to provide detail requested for the CRAMM review is justified at this juncture. A broad estimate of costs will be important to provide feedback to the Cost/Benefit Analysis used to help in selecting the best option

- data assets. The CRAMM reviewer will interview prospective data users and/or the project team to establish information required that cannot be deduced from the Technical Environment Description

Threat Source
An indication of an unwanted incident that could impinge on a system or potential system in some way.

Vulnerability — A weakness of the system and its assets which could be exploited by threats.

… Using CRAMM with SSADM

Index

Application Style Guide, 48
Assemble Feasibility Report (SSADM Step 040), 62, 63
Assemble Requirements Specification (SSADM Step 380), 47
asset groups, 33
asset valuations, 22, 23

Business System Option, 14, 20, 21, 29, 30, 38, 39, 41, 44, 45, 51, 52, 54, 61, 62, 63
Business System Options (SSADM Stage 2), 20, 21, 30, 38, 41, 44, 51, 52, 54, 61, 62, 63

cost, 7, 14, 30, 35, 37, 38, 47, 48, 52, 61, 64
cost/benefit analysis, 38, 47, 61, 64
countermeasures list, 30, 43, 57
CRAMM documentation, 8
CRAMM stage 1, 12, 13, 33, 41
CRAMM stage 2, 13, 35, 42, 52
CRAMM stage 3, 12, 13, 36, 52

data asset, 13, 33, 34, 42, 52, 64
Data Flow Model, 33, 34, 42
Define Business System Options (SSADM Step 210), 38, 61, 62, 63
Define Required System Processing (SSADM Step 310), 44, 64
Define Technical System Options (SSADM Step 410), 48, 62, 63
Define the Problem (SSADM Step 020), 31
Define User Dialogues (SSADM Step 510), 50
Derive Logical View of Current Services (SSADM Step 150), 37, 38
Derive System Functions (SSADM Step 330), 64
Develop Required Data Model (SSADM Step 320), 45

Elementary Process Descriptions, 45
Entity Descriptions, 33, 34, 61
Establish Analysis Framework (SSADM Step 110), 63

Feasibility (SSADM Stage 0), 11, 14, 23, 25, 29, 30, 31, 32, 33, 37, 39, 41, 42, 43, 44, 62, 63

Feasibility Option, 14, 29, 30, 31, 33, 37, 41, 62, 63
Feasibility Report, 31, 62, 63
Feasibility Study, 11, 14, 23, 25, 31, 32, 37, 39, 41, 42, 43, 44, 63
Feasibility Study Module, 32
Financial Accounting Countermeasures, 43
Function Definition, 19, 27, 44

I/O Descriptions, 45
Identify Data Assets, 33, 42
Information Highway, 11, 12
Input/Output Control, 43, 45
Installation Style Guide, 48
Investigation of Current Environment (SSADM Stage 1), 11, 37
investment appraisal, 30, 37

Logical Data Model, 33, 34, 42, 45
Logical Design (SSADM Stage 5), 11, 17, 47
Logical System Specification, 11, 47

management meetings, 20, 37, 43, 54
Management Report, 16, 26, 31, 37, 43, 62

Outline Required Environment Description, 31

PBS, 19
physical asset, 13, 22, 23, 35, 41, 42, 64
Physical Design (SSADM Stage 6), 11, 29, 54, 55
Physical Design Module, 29, 54
physical environment, 24, 51, 54, 55, 61
physical implementation, 11, 12, 17
Prepare for the Feasibility Study (SSADM Step 010), 31
PRINCE, 3, 8, 19, 20, 22, 59
Product Breakdown Structure, 19
Project initiation, 21, 29
project management method, 3, 8, 22
project organisation, 20
project plans, 8
Project schedule, 22, 33

Recommended Countermeasures, 39, 45, 48, 50, 57
Relationship Descriptions, 33, 34
Required System Logical Data Model, 45
Requirements Analysis, 11, 14, 37, 40, 44

Index

Requirements Analysis Module, 14, 37, 40, 44
Requirements Catalogue, 13, 26, 30, 31, 39, 50, 57
Requirements Specification, 11, 14, 27, 38, 46, 47
Requirements Specification Module, 14, 27, 38, 46
Review Boundary, 23, 31, 63
risk analysis, 7, 8, 59
risk management, 8

security analyst, 13
security measures, 7, 14, 57
Security Products, 19
security requirements, 7, 22, 23, 27, 47, 50, 51, 54, 57
security review, 48, 50, 62, 63
security risk, 63
security test, 57
Select Business System Option (SSADM Step 220), 39
Select Feasibility Options (SSADM Step 030), 31, 62, 63
Select Technical System Option (SSADM Step 420), 63
software, 12, 13, 16, 22, 23, 24, 26, 29, 30, 33, 35, 36, 39, 41, 48, 50, 51, 52, 54, 61, 62
software asset, 13, 22, 23
software package, 12, 13, 36
Specification of Requirements (SSADM Stage 3), 11
SSADM Stage 4 (see also Technical System Options), 41, 42

Technical Environment Description, 48, 50, 53, 54, 64
Technical System Option, 11, 14, 17, 29, 30, 35, 41, 42, 47, 48, 50, 51, 52, 53, 62, 63

User Guide, 30, 41, 43
user role, 11, 12, 27, 44
using CRAMM, 20, 22
using PRINCE, 20, 22
using SSADM, 7

Value Data Assets, 42
Value Physical Assets, 35, 42, 52